21st Century Skills Library

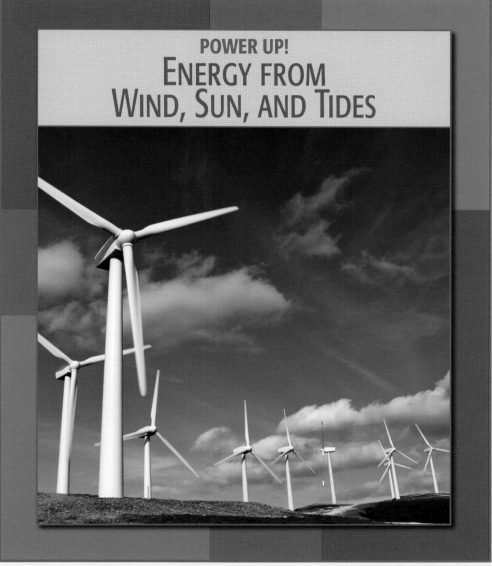

POWER UP!
# ENERGY FROM WIND, SUN, AND TIDES

*Frank Muschal*

**Cherry Lake Publishing**
**Ann Arbor, Michigan**

CHERRY
LAKE
Publishing

Published in the United States of America by Cherry Lake Publishing
Ann Arbor, MI
www.cherrylakepublishing.com

Photo Credits: Page 19, © Shawn Baldwin/Corbis; Page 24, Photo Courtesy of National
Aeronautics and Space Administration (NASA); Page 29, © Photo Courtesy of Verdant
Power, Inc.

Library of Congress Cataloging-in-Publication Data
Muschal, Frank.
  Energy from wind, sun, and tides / Frank Muschal.
      p. cm. — (Power up!)
  Includes index.
  ISBN-13: 978-1-60279-046-9 (lib. bdg.)      978-1-60279-096-4 (pbk.)
  ISBN-10: 1-60279-046-9 (lib. bdg.)          1-60279-096-5 (pbk.)
  1. Wind power—Juvenile literature. 2. Solar power—Juvenile literature.
3. Tidal power—Juvenile literature.  I. Title. II. Series.
  TJ820.M875 2008
  621.31'2136—dc22                              2007005661

Cherry Lake Publishing would like to acknowledge the work of
The Partnership for 21st Century Skills.
Please visit www.21stcenturyskills.org for more information.

## DATE DUE

| | | |
|---|---|---|
| MAR 0 7 2015 | | |
| AUG 0 5 2009 | | |
| MAR 0 7 2013 | | |
| DEC 2 7 2014 | | |
| MAY 1 3 2015 | | |
| | | |
| | | |
| | | |
| | | |
| | | |
| | | |
| | | |
| | | |
| | | |
| | | |
| | | |
| | | |

Demco

# TABLE OF CONTENTS

CHAPTER ONE
Today's Energy Dilemma                              4

CHAPTER TWO
Using Nature to Do the Work                         11

CHAPTER THREE
Energy from Wind                                    15

CHAPTER FOUR
Energy from the Sun                                 21

CHAPTER FIVE
Energy from Tides                                   27


Glossary                                            30

For More Information                                31

Index                                               32

## CHAPTER ONE

# TODAY'S ENERGY DILEMMA

*We use energy to toast the bread, make the coffee, heat the soup, roast the turkey, wash the dishes, and turn on the lights.*

Modern people use a lot of energy. Energy powers our cars, trucks,

trains, and airplanes. Energy keeps us warm in winter and cool in summer.

Energy provides us with light. It allows us to watch television, listen to music, and surf the Internet. Energy cooks our food and keeps it cool.

In the past, many people didn't worry about how much energy they used. Basic needs, such as keeping warm and cooking food, didn't require much fuel. Most people had good supplies of fuel such as trees growing close to their homes. They just cut down nearby forests. This was true for the Pilgrims and other early immigrants. It took many, many years to use up the fuel that the forests provided.

**21st Century Content**

Although most Americans now cook their food on gas or electric stoves, not everyone in the world today is so lucky. Some people in desert environments still use camel dung to cook their meals when no other fuel is available.

**Learning & Innovation Skills**

As the time line in the passage indicates, the world's population is growing faster every year. Why is that the case?

Things are different today. Most Americans no longer cook their food in fireplaces as they did when George Washington was president. There are also many more people alive today than ever before. It took more than 10,000 years for the human population to reach one billion in the early 1800s. It took less than 100 years to increase to two billion. Now, 6.5 billion people live on Earth, each one needing energy resources to live.

About 95 percent of today's energy comes from coal, oil, and gas. These three things are called "fossil fuels." They were formed from the organic remains of prehistoric plants and animals. Over millions

*The remains of prehistoric plants and animals such as these became, over millions of years, fossil fuels we use every day.*

of years, the remains of ancient forests and beasts became buried deep underground. Once there, these dead trees, flowers, dinosaurs, fish, and other plants and animals went through tremendous chemical changes.

One result of these chemical changes was the creation of **petroleum**. Oil companies drill for petroleum all over the world and turn it into gasoline for our cars. Another result of the chemical changes created coal. Electric companies burn coal to make electricity. A third result created natural gas. It is used to heat many homes.

There are main three drawbacks to relying on fossil fuels. First, we are rapidly using some of them up! This is most true of oil because it is not just used to run cars. It is also used to make plastic, paint, and many other everyday products. Some scientists predict that in about 100 years, oil production will fall below the amount that we need.

*Many American oil refineries operate 24 hours a day.*

The second drawback is much more immediate. Burning fossil fuels causes **air pollution**. In some places, people with breathing problems already wear masks when they are outside. Will everyone someday need to wear masks when they go outdoors?

Third, our planet is getting warmer. Burning fossil fuels only makes this worse. This may cause polar ice caps to melt and sea levels to rise. Then cities such as Houston, Miami, and New York could be partly flooded.

## CHAPTER TWO

# USING NATURE TO DO THE WORK

Fortunately, fossil fuels are not the only way to produce energy. For

example, wind power has been used for many centuries.

*Ships on the Nile River have used the same type
of sail for wind power for thousands of years.*

## Wind Power

About 4,000 years ago, Egyptians began using boats with square sails to travel up and down the Nile River. However, these early boats could travel only in the same direction as the wind. Over time, sail **technology** improved. By the 1500s, ships could sail around the world.

*Windmills from the 1800s and before are kept around as remembrances of the past.*

Sailors were among the first to harness the wind, but others soon followed. Windmills were probably first used in what is now Iran even before 700 A.D. These windmills created the energy for grinding grain, sawing wood, and running **looms**. People in Holland became famous for their windmills. These windmills provided energy and also pumped water away from the land so it could be planted with crops. In the 1800s, many American farmers used windmills to pump water out of the ground.

## 21st Century Content

Water, water, water! Although more than half the planet is covered in water, most of it cannot be used by humans to drink or grow plants. That's because most of it is salt water. That's what is found in all the oceans and seas. Only lakes, rivers, and streams have fresh water, which is what we use to drink and grow things. And fresh water is in short supply. Salt water can be turned into fresh water, but the process is way too expensive to be practical—yet.

Another source of energy is waterpower. Watermills built alongside rivers use the rushing water to do the same tasks as windmills. However, watermills are more reliable than windmills, since wind doesn't blow constantly. Watermills powered machines at the start of the **Industrial Revolution**. In the early 1800s, for example, watermills provided energy for the woolen mills in Lowell, Massachusetts.

## CHAPTER THREE

# ENERGY FROM WIND

*Windmills are still used to pump water for cattle and other livestock.*

Windmills have long been used to grind grain and pump water.

However, they were mostly replaced in the early 1900s by electrical plants

that could generate a great deal more power by burning coal. Now, though, windmills are making a comeback!

Of course, single windmills still aren't powerful enough to make large amounts of electricity. Much larger—and more—windmills are needed. That's exactly what are being built now around the planet.

In the past, windmills were only three or four stories tall. However, windmills today are huge! They can be 15 stories tall or more, and this is just for the base. The blades of today's windmills are huge as well. Each of the three blades of a modern windmill may be 40 feet (12.2 meters) long. That's longer than

a three-story building is tall. The new windmills are
so huge that several large flatbed trucks are needed to
move the parts of just one of them.

Even though they are huge, modern windmills
work best when there are a lot of them. Sometimes,
dozens of windmills are erected in the same area.
Then you have a **wind farm**. Having 40 or more
windmills in a wind farm is common. The Altamont
Pass area of California has about 7,000 windmills.
Now that's really a lot! Some companies in California
even offer tours of local wind farms.

Making the best possible use of the energy we now have is also important. Think about your energy use in the past few days. Have you left unneeded lights burning? Have you turned the thermostat up or down instead of dressing for the temperature? How can you do your part to conserve and make better use of the energy now available?

*Tests have shown that seacoasts are a good place for wind farms due to the steady velocity of coastal breezes.*

Of course, wind farms do best in windy areas. Sometimes, these are in

vast, open areas, such as the plains of the Midwest. The winds there are

fairly constant. Right now, there are big wind farms in California, Iowa,

New Mexico, New Jersey, and other states. Japan, India, Germany, and

Australia have wind farms, too. Another good place is on the seacoasts,

where winds are pretty constant, too.

*The people of India willingly deal with the monsoon's flooding
to get the benefits the essential rainfall brings to farmers.*

However, local people sometimes object to having a wind farm nearby.

People in Ireland objected to more wind farms after one there caused an

enormous landslide. The huge windmills were too heavy for the ground

they had been built on, and the land collapsed. In India, **monsoon** rains

have been essential to life for thousands of years and bring up to

90 percent of the yearly rainfall. When the monsoon rains were poor, some people blamed the 1,700 windmills in one region.

People have protested American wind farms, too. A few years ago, an energy company planned to build 130 windmills more than 40 stories tall off Cape Cod in Massachusetts. Many protestors demanded that the project not be built, saying it would harm the area's famous ocean views. In California, protestors went to court to have some windmills removed. Birds in the area, including some golden eagles, had been killed when they flew into the slowly spinning blades.

## CHAPTER FOUR

# Energy from the Sun

*Every 24 hours, the Sun comes up and begins another
cycle of radiating enormous energy down on Earth.*

The Sun is an enormous source of energy. If you ever got a sunburn,

you know this is true! The Sun has burned for billions of years and will

continue to do so for billions more. Enough sunlight falls on the Earth's

surface in an hour to meet the world's energy needs for a year. Today, scientists are finding ways to make **solar** energy an efficient, cost-effective power resource.

## Solar-Powered Today

Already, we are using solar-powered tools, and we may not even realize it. Many people have small, solar-powered calculators. They are inexpensive to buy, and they never need batteries. Solar energy also supplies the power for some radios, flashlights, and fans. Manufacturers are even beginning to make solar-powered refrigerators and freezers. These are all good uses for solar power, but they provide only small amounts of energy overall.

## Solar-Powered Homes

Most homes today use lots of electricity. Now some homeowners are installing solar panels to provide some or all of this electrical power. These solar panels can cut electricity bills in half. The town of

*Solar panels work best in regions with lots of strong sunlight, such as Arizona.*

Clarum, California, already has 257 houses powered with solar energy.

The town wants to become the largest community in California to

generate as much electricity as it uses.

*The International Space Station is largely powered*
*by several long rows of solar panels.*

## Out of This World Energy

The International Space Station uses solar panels as its main source of electricity. And this electricity does more than just turn on the lights! It also provides the energy to contact Earth, do experiments, and just plain live. Without the solar panels, crew members would quickly freeze to death.

The station circles Earth almost 16 times a day. When it is on the nighttime side of Earth, it uses the solar energy it has stored in batteries.

**21st Century Content**

Companies are working to expand the use of solar energy. Although there are about 10,000 homes in the U.S. entirely powered by solar energy, over 60% of the solar technology sales are exports to developing countries.

## Solar Power Plants

Solar panels are now being used for more than just individual homes. They are being used to create large amounts of electricity. One such solar power plant is in the Mojave Desert in California. Several others are in Europe. And these plants can be very, very big. One solar plant in Germany has 33,000 solar panels in it! We can expect to see more and more solar power plants in the future.

## CHAPTER FIVE

# ENERGY FROM TIDES

Another source for energy may be ocean tides. One big advantage is that tides are very predictable. Even a thousand years ago, tidal mills were used to grind flour in Europe. However, things have not progressed much in all that time because the technology is expensive. Large-scale, costly

*The power of tides, as they go in and out, can move boats such as this far up the beach.*

engineering is required to tap the potential energy of the tides. Once the project is in place, however, tidal power is very cheap.

## Using Tides

Rising and falling tides can be used to create power. When the tide comes in, it flows through **sluice gates** into a natural or man-made **basin**. Then the sluice gates are closed, holding the water in the basin. As the sea level drops during low tide, the sluice gates control the water as it flows back out. The force of the moving water is used to create electricity.

*The East River turbine project may someday provide electricity for a significant portion of New York City.*

## Another Tide System

In 2007, another type of tidal system began testing in New York City's East River. This system uses underwater **turbines**. They rotate very slowly as tides flow in and out. In fact, the turbines move so slowly that they will not harm any fish in the area. Still, each turbine creates enough electricity to power one home. For now, though, there are just a few turbines.

Someday, however, there may be hundreds!

# GLOSSARY

**air pollution (air puh-LOO-shuhn)** unhealthy things such as smoke, dust, and fumes in the atmosphere

**basin (BEY-suhn)** depression in the Earth's surface that holds a large volume of water

**Industrial Revolution [in-DUHS-tree-uhl rev-uh-LOO-shuhn]** historical period starting in the late 1700s when large-scale factory production began

**looms (looms)** machines that weave cloth

**monsoon (mon-SOON)** very strong, seasonal wind pattern

**petroleum (puh-TROH-lee-uhm)** thick, flammable material that occurs naturally under the ground and can be turned into gasoline and other products

**sluice gates (sloos geyts)** devices to control the flow of large amounts of water

**solar (SOH-ler)** of or relating to the Sun

**technology (tek-NOL-uh-jee)** tools and techniques for carrying out industrial plans

**turbines (TUR-bins)** machines with blades or paddles that turn to produce energy when a fluid flows over them

**wind farm (wind fahrm)** area with many modern windmills

# FOR MORE INFORMATION

## BOOKS

Coughlan, John. *Green Cars: Earth-Friendly Electric Vehicles.*
Mankato, MN: Capstone Press, 1994.

Levete, Sarah. *Solar Power.*
North Mankato, MN: Stargazer Books, 2006.

Macaulay, David. *Mill.* Boston: Houghton Mifflin, 1983.

Miller, Kimberly. *What If We Run Out of Fossil Fuels?*
New York: Children's Press, 2002.

Petersen, Christine. *Alternative Energy.*
New York: Children's Press, 2004.

Petersen, Christine. *Water Power.* New York: Children's Press, 2004.

Rogers, Daniel. *Waves, Tides and Currents.*
New York: Bookwright Press, 1991.

Walker, Niki. *Generating Wind Power.*
New York: Crabtree Publishing, 2007.

## Other Media

*The Engine Counts.* DVD. Varied Directions, 2006.

*Global Warming: The Signs and the Science.* DVD. PBS, 2005.

*NOVA: "World in the Balance: The Population Paradox."*
DVD. WGBH, Boston, 2004.

To find out more about how electricity is made, see:
*http://www.eia.doe.gov/kids/energyfacts/sources/electricity.html*

# INDEX

air pollution, 10

basin, 28

camel dung, 5
cars, 4
coal, 6–8, 16
cooking fuel, 5–6, 23

Egyptians, 12
electric companies, 8
electrical plant, 15
electricity, 8, 16, 23–26,
    28–29
energy conservation, 17

fossil fuels, 6–10, 11

gasoline, 8
golden eagles, 20

heat, 8
Herschel, John, 22
human population, 6

Industrial Revolution, 14
International Space Station,
    24–25

looms, 13
Lowell mills, 14

monsoon rains, 19–20

National Mills Weekend, 16

natural gas, 5, 8

oil, 6, 8, 9
oil companies, 8

petroleum, 8
Pilgrims, 5
polar bears, 10
polar ice caps, 10

sails, 11,12
sea level, 10, 28
sluice gates, 28
solar energy, 22–26
solar panels, 23–26
solar power
    homes, 23–25
    plants, 26
    tools, 22–23
Sun, 21
sunlight, 22

technology, 12, 27
tidal mills, 27
tides
    as energy source, 27–29
    high and low, 28

underwater turbines, 29

warm weather, 10
water pumps, 13, 15
watermills, 14

waterpower, 14, 28
wind, 12–13, 15, 17
wind farm, 17–20
wind power, 11–13
windmills, 12–13, 15–20

## ABOUT THE AUTHOR

**Frank Muschal** lives in Chicago with his elderly cat, Agatha. ("She's older than laptops and cell phones, but I'm older than TV.") He's been writing and editing for textbook publishers for thirty years and has no guilt feelings about tormenting students all that time. Besides writing, Frank keeps busy playing tennis, riding horses, and fumbling around on his guitar. "I'm no rock star," he says. "I just want to make me more interesting to myself."